TABLE OF CONTENTS

ACRONYMS

CBRNE	Chemical, Biological, Radiological, Nuclear, and High-Explosive
COCOM	Combatant Commander
DHS	Department of Homeland Security
DoD	Department of Defense
DSCA	Defense Support to Civil Authorities
FEMA	Federal Emergency Management Agency
GAO	United States Government Accountability Office
GCC	Geographic Combatant Commander
NORAD	North American Aerospace Defense Command
PDD	Presidential Decision Directive
USNORTHCOM	United States Northern Command

ILLUSTRATIONS

CHAPTER 1

INTRODUCTION

All this means that the integrating function of U.S. policymaking processes will be challenged as never before. Traditional national security agencies (State, Defense, CIA, NSC staff) will need to work together in new ways, and economic agencies (Treasury, Commerce, U.S. Trade Representative) will need to work more closely with the traditional national security community. In addition, other players–especially Justice and Transportation–will need to be integrated more fully into national security processes. Merely improving the interagency process around present structures may not suffice.
— Hart Rudman Commission, *Seeking a National Strategy*

A Brief Discussion of Homeland Security

The American style of government is a federal system wherein the governmental responsibilities of the United States are shared between the state and national levels. The 10th Amendment to the *United States Constitution* explicitly reserves all powers not granted by the Constitution to the federal government for exercise by the states. Therefore, state governors and the federal government share responsibility for ensuring their citizen's safety and security resulting in the distribution and decentralizing of capabilities and responsibilities.[1] This division of governmental responsibilities places constraints on the collective governmental ability to provide security for America and the defense of her citizens.

The *Goldwater Nichols Act of 1986* established the Geographical Combatant Commands (GCC), which are directly subordinate to the Secretary of Defense. The GCCs are delineated geographically or functionally by the President through the Unified Command Plan. Every GCC is commanded by a Combatant Commander (COCOM) who is responsible for the conduct of military operations that affect their stipulated areas of

1

responsibility. A common thread between the various GCCs it that every COCOM is charged with advancement of the national interests of the United States as expressed in the *National Security Strategy*, *National Defense Strategy*, and *National Military Strategy of the United States*. These strategic documents clearly define that the number one priority for each GCC is the security of the United States and its citizens.

The terrorist attacks of 11 September 2001 graphically and definitively demonstrated that the United States faced new security threats that existing structures were not designed to confront. The governmental systems, policies, and structures of the United States in place on 11 September 2001 were conceived during the Cold War and relied upon the premise of mutually assured destruction. Therefore, these structures were designed to confront an enemy that was no longer the predominant threat to the United States in the years following the end of the Cold War. The security of the United States had changed from one of mutually assured destruction to one of global unity based upon mutually assured dependence.[2] The attacks of 11 September 2001 clearly revealed the fundamentally changed nature of the threats faced by the United States and the resultant shortcomings of the institutions responsible for the safety and security of the nation's citizens.

The terrorist attacks of 11 September 2001 provided the impetus for a series of governmental reorganizations and changes in order to adapt to the post Cold War security environment. One of the many changes to the governmental systems, policies, and structures was realized through the passing of the *Homeland Security Act of 2002*. The *Homeland Security Act of 2002* established the Department of Homeland Security (DHS) as an executive department of the United States under Title 5, United States Code. The passage of the *Homeland Security Act of 2002* and the subsequent establishment of the DHS is "the most extensive reorganization of the federal government in the past fifty years."[3]

The DHS is a headquarters framework with the charter to prevent and disrupt terrorist attacks within the United States; protect the American people, critical infrastructure, and key resources; respond and recover from incidents that do occur, and set the foundation to ensure our long term success.[4] DHS seeks to achieve greater unity of purpose for overlapping federal, state, and local jurisdictions encompassing 22 separate federal agencies, all 50 state governments, and over 87,000 different local jurisdictions.[5] The federal agencies involved include the Transportation Security Administration, U.S. Customs and Border Protection, U.S. Citizenship and Immigration Services, U.S. Immigration and Customs Enforcement, Secret Service, Federal Emergency Management Agency (FEMA), and the United States Coast Guard.[6] The mandate for DHS is all encompassing and wide ranging from the federal to the local level.

On 1 October 2002 United States Northern Command (USNORTHCOM) was established as a GCC by order of the President. The establishment of USNORTHCOM addressed the lack of unity of effort between the federal (active duty and reserve) and state (National Guard) DoD elements assigned to conduct homeland defense, homeland security, and Defense Support to Civil Authorities (DSCA) missions. USNORTHCOM became the lead agent for DoD efforts when conducting DSCA operations.[7]

In recognition of the unique coordination and interoperability challenges posed to USNORTHCOM, the original development study team drafted staffing guidelines that called for approximately 500 personnel. Half of these personnel were to be active duty and the other half from the National Guard. The National Guard personnel were to provide the requisite expertise for integration with state governors and their associated security personnel and apparatus. The staffing also called for intergovernmental staffing solutions that included non-DoD leadership positions to facilitate the intergovernmental coordination and federal to state collaboration necessary to support DSCA.[8]

The provision for non-DoD leadership within USNORTHCOM reinforces the whole of government approach to homeland security and defense envisioned by the *Homeland Security Act of 2002*. The incorporation of federal, state, and intergovernmental agencies within the permanent organization of USNORTHCOM is unique among GCCs and indicative of the unique geography in which USNORTHCOM operates.

State governors also embraced their responsibilities as state executives in the days after 11 September 2001. As discussed previously, federalist design of the government dictates that governors have the dominant voice when addressing issues and concerns within the borders of their states. Consequently, many state governors hired their own homeland security advisors and began to develop methods to secure their citizens; turning to their National Guard units to provide the military expertise required.[9] In exercising their Constitutional responsibilities, state governors have added another level of complexity to the task of providing homeland security as well as additional requirements and challenges to the National Guard formations within their states.

Admiral Mike Mullen, the former Chairman of the Joint Chiefs of Staff, identified the burgeoning national debt as the greatest national security threat facing the United

States.[10] We have already seen limited efforts to reduce the growth of the national deficit through the adjustment of federal agency budgets. It is reasonable to expect that the reduction of resources available to provide for homeland security will necessitate an accompanying adjustment of the apparatus providing that security.

The current homeland security design relies upon multiple levels of federal and state agencies spread between the DoD and DHS, as well as state emergency management organizations. These multiple levels of agencies and organizations result in redundant means with regard to homeland security. While redundancy provides robustness to the system, it must be by design and with sound reasoning to justify the expenditure of the means necessary to create and sustain said redundancy. As resource levels decrease because of budgetary pressure, the relationship between the DoD and DHS to provide homeland security may need to be adjusted.

Research Question

Does the current organization of DoD and DHS best achieve homeland security in a time of diminishing resources?

Secondary Research Questions

The secondary questions I am asking are what are the DoD responsibilities and obligations for homeland security? What functions does DHS perform to ensure homeland security? What responsibilities are held at the state level with regard to homeland security?

Scope and Limitations

There were several limitations to this study. First, the amount of time and resources available to conduct the research was limited. Therefore, conclusions may have been subject to unintentional bias or errors of omission through the selection of the sources utilized to conduct this study. Secondly, the literature review was limited to materials that can be obtained or referenced locally through the Combined Arms Research Library utilizing interlibrary loan or electronic methods. Third, the scope of this study only addressed resources and events prior to 1 April 2012. Fourth, this study focused on the issues of homeland security from the American perspective without addressing or speculating on any potential international relations impacts. Lastly, the continual evolution of the mechanisms of homeland security will continue which may render the conclusion(s) and recommendation(s) of this study no longer applicable.

Delimitations

This study did not propose exact legislative or legal language but rather focused on the strategic level concepts, policies, and themes that resulted from the analysis of the subject. Additionally, this study did not address fiscal projections in order to make quantitative assessments but utilized the assumption that multiple entities with similar responsibly inherently require more resources than one entity exercising the same number of responsibilities.

Relevance

The relevance of this research was based on several assumptions about the enduring external threat environment to the United States and the continual need to defend against them. The first assumption was that a credible threat to the United States is still posed by threats operating in the air, sea, space, land, and cyberspace that could potentially inflict enormous physical and psychological damage upon the homeland. The second assumption was that the tide of globalization will not ebb which will allow state and non-state actors to access and attack the United States. The third assumption was that the United States will have to assure her security with ever decreasing resources and increasing threats. The United States is currently carrying a national debt in excess of $14 trillion dollars; to expect continued government spending on homeland security to be unaffected by fiscal constraint is not a valid assumption.

This research is significant because it provides an analysis of how to ensure homeland security within the economic realities of shrinking homeland security budgets. This research shows that the ways and means of achieving homeland security cannot remain static in the face of the new economic challenges and uncertainty while the ends remain the same. The aim was to answer the most fundamental homeland security question of the day; how can we achieve homeland security in a time of decreasing national resources?

Closing

The purpose of this thesis was to determine if the current organization of DoD and DHS best achieves homeland security in a time of diminishing resources.

---

[1]Kristine L. Shelstad, "The Domestic Security Command–The Evolution of the U.S. Northern Command" (Master's Thesis, Naval Postgraduate School, Monterrey, CA, 2011), 5.

[2]Stephen Vrooman, "Homeland Security Strategy from the Cold War into the Global War on Terrorism: An Analysis of Deterrence, Forward Presence, and Homeland

Defense" (Master's Thesis, U.S. Army. Command and General Staff College, Ft. Leavenworth, KS, 2004), 5.

[3]U.S. Department of Homeland Security, *National Strategy for Homeland Security* (Washington, DC: Government Printing Office, July 2002), https://www.hsdl.org/homesec/docs/dhs/nps17-090605-05.pdf (accessed 2 December 2011), vii.

[4]U.S. Department of Homeland Security, *National Strategy for Homeland Security* (Washington, DC: Government Printing Office, October 2007), http://www.dhs.gov/xabout/history/gc_1193938363680.shtm (accessed 2 December 2011), 1.

[5]U.S. Department of Homeland Security, *National Strategy for Homeland Security*, July 2002, 11.

[6]U.S. Department of Homeland Security, *Homeland Security Organizational Chart* (Washington, DC: Government Printing Office), http://www.dhs.gov/xabout/structure/editorial_0644.shtm (accessed 2 December 2011).

[7]Shelstad, 6.

[8]Ibid., 7.

[9]Ibid., 6.

[10]Michael J. Carden, "National Debt Poses Security Threat, Mullen Says," *American Forces Press Services*, 26 August 2010, www.jcs.mil/newsarticle.aspx?ID=360 (accessed 24 January 2012).

CHAPTER 2

LITERATURE REVIEW

Taken together, the evidence suggests that threats to American security will be more diffuse, harder to anticipate, and more difficult to neutralize that ever before. Deterrence will not work as it once did; in many cases it may not work at all. There will be a blurring of the boundaries: between homeland defense and foreign policy; between sovereign states and a plethora of protectorates and autonomous zones; between the pull of national loyalties on individual citizens and the pull of loyalties both more local and more global in nature.

— Hart Rudman Commission, *New World Coming*

Introduction

This review provides a brief history of the governmental design and evolutionary nature of the structures that comprise the homeland security design of the United States. It endeavors to convey the overall theme of a nation that is reticent to employ military forces within its own borders and relies on the local and state governments to exercise the responsibilities placed on them by the *10th Amendment* of the *United States Constitution*.

Governmental Design

The framers of the Constitution developed a federalist system of government that utilizes a division of powers between the federal and state governments. This division of powers is also known as checks and balances to prevent one level or branch of government from exercising unchecked powers. The division of responsibilities between the federal and state governments is codified in the *10th Amendment* to the *United States Constitution*. The *10th Amendment* reserves all powers not granted by the *Constitution* to the Federal government for exercise by the states.[1] The *10th Amendment* creates tension between the federal and state executives when attempting to provide for the security of their citizens. The *10th Amendment* does not prohibit military involvement in activities within the United States but it does limit what kind of operations can be conducted by federal troops within the United States. The limiting of domestic military operations, to those necessary to provide for the common defense, was a result of the American experience with British military abuses which sowed some of the seeds that resulted in the Revolutionary War. The *10th Amendment* does not restrict federal troops from conducting domestic law enforcement type operations; this restriction was imposed by Congress following the Civil War during the period known as Reconstruction.

In the Reconstruction Era, the federal army was used to perform law enforcement operations across the recently defeated Confederate States of America. The use of federal troops to impose law and order was a matter of necessity as the law enforcement institutions across the defeated Confederacy were disbanded and rule of law was in question. The use of federal troops to impose law and order across the defeated confederacy effectively placed the powers of the judiciary under the executive branch, a dangerous violation of the checks and balances design of the Constitution. Congress subsequently passed the *Posse Comitatus Act* to prevent future usurpation of the powers of the judiciary with military forces. The *Posse Comitatus Act* prevents federal troops from being used for domestic law enforcement unless expressly authorized by the *Constitution* or an Act of Congress.[2]

The interpretation of the *Posse Comitatus Act* has evolved as the military has changed since Reconstruction. The federal army is now equivalent to the Title 10 active duty force and the state militia has been replaced by the Title 32 National Guard formations. Title 10 and Title 32 are the budget authorization categories provided by

Congress to differentiate between federal and state forces. Title 32 forces can be federalized by Presidential authorization which transfers them to Title 10 status. *Posse Comitatus* is therefore understood to apply to forces under Title 10 budgetary authority which includes all active duty forces and federalized National Guard forces. Therefore, state executives are not barred by the *Posse Comitatus Act* from using their National Guard formations to conduct law enforcement activities within their jurisdictions as long as they remain under Title 32 budgetary authority. While *Posse Comitatus* restricts the utilization of federal troops domestically, the *Insurrection Act* authorizes the use of federal troops under specific circumstances.

The *Insurrection Acts* states:

> Whenever the President considers that unlawful obstructions, combinations, or assemblages, or rebellion against the authority of the United States, make it impracticable to enforce the laws of the United States in any State by the ordinary course of judicial proceedings, he may call into Federal service such of the militia of any State, and use such of the armed forces, as he considers necessary to enforce those laws or to suppress the rebellion.[3]

The *Insurrection Act* has been enacted three times by Executive order. The *Insurrection Act* was first utilized in 1957 by President Eisenhower when he dispatched federal troops to enforce the integration of public schools in Arkansas following the landmark Brown versus Board of Education decision by the United States Supreme Court. President Johnson used the *Insurrection Act* again in the 1960s when he utilized federal troops to reestablish the rule of law in Alabama following the race riots. The most recent utilization of the *Insurrection Act* occurred in 1992 when the widespread violence that erupted following the Rodney King verdict exceeded local law enforcement capabilities to reestablish the rule of law.

11

While government agencies may utilize the resources of other agencies, their utilization is constrained by the *Economy Act*. The *Economy Act* requires that any government agency receiving goods or services from another government agency will reimburse the provider of the goods or services in advance or upon delivery.[4] Therefore, any governmental agency that leverages military capabilities or resources must reimburse the DoD for the cost associated therein.

The *Stafford Act* further limits the use of federal forces to conduct domestic operations by placing the responsibility for emergency planning on the state and local governments. "It is the intent of the Congress, by this Act [Stafford Act], to provide an orderly and continuing means of assistance by the Federal Government to State and local governments in carrying out their responsibilities to alleviate the suffering and damage which result from disasters."[5]

Homeland Security during the Cold War

The United States emerged from World War II with enormous military capability and capacity. The military that fought and won World War II was not the military force necessary to ensure the peace. The crushing burden of debt incurred during World War II and the enormous costs associated with maintaining the force necessitated the reduction of the American military. In 1947, President Truman signed the *National Security Act of 1947*, which was the first attempt at "a comprehensive program for the future security of the United States; to provide for the establishment of integrated policies and procedures for the departments, agencies, and functions of the Government relating to the national security."[6] The *National Security Act of 1947* endeavored to provide for the future security of the nation through several institutional design changes.

The National Security Act of 1947, subsequently amended in 1949 and 1952, established the National Security Council to integrate all the elements of national power into a single entity responsible for providing recommendations to the President on matters of national security. It also established the DoD and the Joint Chiefs of Staff. The DoD combined the functions of the Secretary of War and Department of War into one civilian organization with one seat on the President's cabinet. The Joint Chiefs of Staff was established to provide military advice and counsel to the newly established DoD. The United States Air Force was also established as an independent military service, on par with the United States Army and Navy. The establishment of an independent Air Force was a direct reflection of the changing nature of the threat to national security through aerial warfare.

The United States relied primarily upon geographic isolation and force projection for homeland defense until the 1950s. The development and fielding of intercontinental bombers and ballistic missiles shrank the world and geographic isolation was no longer a viable defense against external attack. To address the newly emerged threat from intercontinental weapons a new military command was established in cooperation with the Canadians, the North American Aerospace Defense Command (NORAD). NORAD became the only military command with direct responsibility for defense of the United States within its borders.

In 1986 the *Goldwater Nichols Act* was passed resulting in a massive reorganization of the DoD. *Goldwater Nichols* relegated the service chiefs to advisory roles and squarely established the military chain of command as running from the President, to the Secretary of Defense, and directly to the newly established GCCs and their respective COCOMs. The Unified Command Plan enacted by the President divided the world into four geographical GCCs but the territorial confines of the United States were not assigned to a GCC. *Goldwater Nichols* further reinforced that the United States was focused outward to provide homeland defense.

Status Quo between the Cold War and 11 September 2001

With the fall of the Berlin Wall and the subsequent collapse of the Soviet Union, the United States was left as the last remaining superpower. Some went so far as to refer to the United States as the first hyper power because of her unmatched ability to rapidly project military power across the span of the globe. While America struggled to define the strategic mechanisms to guide international relations a new threat was on the horizon. Terrorism was not a new threat or idea, but its application was evolving and increasing in lethality through the harnessing of the advances of globalization. The United States was not the only target for terrorist attacks, terrorism became a global phenomenon.

Globalization fundamentally changed the methods and speed with which the world interacts, resulting "in a much more inter-connected world with unprecedented freedom of movement."[7] Terrorists seized the advantages provided by the freedom of movement of people, goods, and ideas afforded by the interconnected transportation and communications systems of globalization. These super-empowered individuals, regimes, and ideologies have the ability to threaten the security of the United States from the farthest corners of the earth without having discernible and easily targeted centers of gravity as they exist without nation state type structures to target.[8]

In 1993 the World Trade Center was attacked by foreign extremists. Recognizing the limitations of the existing Cold War era national security design, President Bill

14

Clinton signed *Presidential Decision Directive (PDD) 39* in June 1995 which defined the United States policy "to deter, defeat and respond vigorously to all terrorist attacks on our territory and against our citizens, or facilities, whether they occur domestically, in international waters or airspace or on foreign territory."[9] *PDD-39* established the policy of actively seeking extradition of terrorists from foreign soil either diplomatically or unilaterally through use of force. *PDD-39* charged the DoD with lead agency responsibilities for domestic counterterrorism as well as establishing interagency teams to ensure that a whole of government approach was applied to homeland defense and security. *PDD-39* was the first document to identify the prevention of terrorist groups acquiring weapons of mass destruction as the highest national priority.

In 1996 the *Nunn-Lugar-Domenici Domestic Preparedness Program Act* was passed by Congress. This act tasked the DoD to provide local and state first responders with the specialized skills necessary to respond to domestic weapons of mass destruction incidents or attacks. The Nunn-Lugar-Domenici Commission continued to investigate the threats posed by weapons of mass destruction. The DoD led the resulting program, but heavily leveraged the unique capabilities of the Federal Bureau of Investigation and the Federal Emergency Management Agency to build an interagency team. Congress appropriated funds to allow local and state first responders to procure equipment and receive specialized training to respond to weapons of mass destruction incidents. These federal funds provided increased capabilities to the existing state and local emergency preparedness programs instead of establishing a new organization.

In July 1998, the US Commission on National Security/21st Century, also known as the Hart-Rudman Commission, began work to determine what structures were necessary to ensure national security requirements into the next century.[10] In September 1999, they issued the first of three eventual reports in which they assessed that the United States was still vulnerable to attack and the existing security structures were not sufficient to address the newly emerging threats to the United States. The Hart-Rudman Commission issued their second report in April 2000 and their final report in February 2001.

While the work of the Hart-Rudman Commission was ongoing the DoD established Joint Task Force Civil Support. Joint Task Force Civil Support was an intergovernmental effort between DoD and the Federal Emergency Management Agency to conduct planning for their combined response to domestic disasters and national emergencies. DoD also established Weapons of Mass Destruction Civil Support Teams in the Army and Air National Guard. These teams were designed to provide chemical, biological, and nuclear expertise to state and federal agencies in all 50 states.

The Hart-Rudman Commission recommended many changes to the national security structures of the United States. The Commission recommended creating a DoD Assistant for Homeland Security to oversee all DoD activities within the domestic arena. The Commission also recognized the primacy of the National Guard to provide for defense type capabilities and resources within the confines of the United States. The Hart-Rudman Commission linked the federalist design of the Constitution and subsequent legislation to recommend the reorientation of the National Guard towards homeland security. In the final report of the Commission they prophetically warned that a major direct attack by terrorists on American soil was likely.

11 September 2001 Changes the Homeland Security Design

The attacks of 11 September 2001 changed the way America thought about homeland security and defense. For the first time in nearly 60 years, the United States was directly attacked resulting in thousands of deaths on American soil. Unlike the Pearl Harbor attack, the 11 September 2001 attack was perpetrated by a terrorist organization, not a nation state. America was attacked by the kind of enemy envisioned by the Hart Rudman Commission. America's primary threat to homeland security was any super-empowered individual, regime, or ideology that is "dangerously disconnected from the globalizing world, from its rule sets, its norms, and all the ties that bind countries together."[11]

In July 2002 the inaugural *National Strategy for Homeland Security* was published in the aftermath of 11 September 2001. The *National Strategy for Homeland Security* called for the establishment of a system that enabled integration and collaboration on a national scale. It relied heavily on state and local governments and capabilities to respond to incidents. Additionally, it detailed civil and military roles and responsibilities in a number of predicted emergency response scenarios. This national strategy set the stage for major legislation to be passed later in the year.

The DoD and Congress both made major changes to the way homeland security and homeland defense were conducted in 2002. Congress passed, and the President signed the *Homeland Security Act of 2002* on 25 September 2002 which established the DHS. The goal for DHS was to merge 22 different federal organizations to provide a unified structure for homeland security operations. DHS was responsible for protecting the homeland, borders, ports, critical infrastructure; coordinating communication between federal, state, and local governments; synthesizing intelligence critical to homeland security; and keeping the public informed.

DHS was initially given responsibility, but not the authority, to make changes. Major shortcomings were the division of responsibilities between the Department of Justice and the nascent DHS, interface between DHS and DoD, and the lack of an intelligence capability in DHS.

DoD recommended, and the President approved the establishment of a GCC with responsibility for the United States, its territories, and territorial waters. This new GCC was called USNORTHCOM and officially assumed responsibility for United States territory on 1 October 2002. USNORTHCOM's mission was to deter, prevent, preempt, and defeat threats and aggression aimed at the United States. When directed by the National Command Authority, it would provide military assistance to civil authorities, consequence management operations, and protect and defend the United States.[12] The original manning documents for USNORTHCOM called for a robust intergovernmental structure as well as heavy reliance on the domestic capabilities and expertise provided by the National Guard.

Homeland Security Presidential Directive 5 was signed by the President in 2003; it named the DHS Secretary as the principal federal official responsible for domestic incident management. It clarified that DHS would lead intergovernmental efforts with respect to homeland security. *Homeland Security Presidential Directive 5* also dictated that a *National Response Plan* would be produced by DHS to integrate a whole of government response to domestic incidents. *Homeland Security Presidential Directive 8* followed a few months later which provided planning and preparation guidance for homeland security response as well as providing detailed guidance to the DoD on specific enabling capabilities they were responsible for providing to civil authorities. *Homeland Security Presidential Directive 8* also amended the *Homeland Security Presidential Directive 5* language to reflect a more offensive mindset in the preparation for and prevention of the management of domestic incidents.

In 2004, the *National Response Plan* was published in accordance with *Homeland Security Presidential Directive 5*. The plan clarified federal roles and responsibilities as well as reinforcing the importance of local and state agencies for providing for the security and responding to incidents. Federal, civilian, and military forces would still be available for collaboration as well as response to incidents of national significance.

The Chairman of the Joint Chiefs of Staff published an updated *National Military Strategy* in 2004. A major emphasis of the strategy was DoD support for civil authorities at the federal, state, and local level when the nature of the incident exceeds their capability to respond. The *National Defense Strategy* of 2005 reinforced that DoD support to civil authorities would occur when first responders were overwhelmed. Additionally, the 2005 *National Defense Strategy* emphasized that DoD capabilities to move large amounts of men and material quickly was critical to support of homeland security and domestic incident response.

In June 2005 the *Strategy for Homeland Defense and Civil Support* was published by the DoD. USNORTHCOM was designed as the lead planner for the active, reserve, and National Guard forces that would be part of the intergovernmental response to a domestic incident. The strategy relied heavily on the ability of the National Guard to provide the civil to military interface at the local and state level. A role they have traditionally played in their Title 32 capacity. The identification of National Guard forces to conduct domestic operations in support of the national response deftly threaded the nuanced federal laws that restrict domestic military operations.

The *National Strategy for Homeland Security* was updated in October 2007. This update addresses the changes in our understanding of the terrorist threat since the inaugural strategy as well as capturing the lessons learned from domestic crises such as Hurricane Katrina.[13]

In 2008 Congress included language in the *National Defense Authorization Act* providing for the establishment of a Council of Governors to advise the Secretary of Defense. In January 2011 the President issued an executive order establishing the Council of Governors. The Council of Governors was intended to provide a forum for governors to provide feedback and advice to the Secretary of Defense on DoD actions and policies with direct impacts upon their states.[14]

In February 2009, *Presidential Study Directive One* was signed which directed the Assistant to the President for Homeland Security and Counterterrorism to perform an interagency review with the intent of strengthening the government's strategic planning capability. Additionally, it seeks ideas to seamlessly integrate domestic and international efforts to achieve homeland security by combating international terrorism, organized crime, narco-trafficking, and domestic incidents (hurricanes, floods, fires, etc). It also rescinded *National Security Presidential Directive 8* (NSPD-8).

Presidential Policy Directive 8 was issued on 30 March 2011. It declared "our national preparedness is the shared responsibility of all levels of government, the private and nonprofit sectors, and individual citizens."[15] *Presidential Policy Directive 8* was intended to galvanize action by the Federal Government to facilitate an "all-of-Nation, capabilities-based approach to preparedness."[16] *Presidential Policy Directive 8* charged the Secretary of DHS to establish a national preparedness goal which would be facilitated by a national preparedness system with the overarching goal of building and sustaining an all-of-Nation cycle of preparedness activities including resource and personnel guidance as well as equipment aimed at nationwide interoperability. *Presidential Policy Directive 8* also rescinded *Homeland Security Presidential Directive 8*.

In testimony before the Senate Armed Service Committee on 13 March 2012, General Charles H. Jacoby, Jr., the USNORTHCOM Commander outlined the areas in which USNORTHCOM is adjusting their operations in order to better conduct civil support operations. The initiatives he highlighted are the expansion of the Dual-Status Commander concept, implementation of a new Chemical, Biological, Radiological, and Nuclear (CBRN) Response Enterprise, and new authority granted to the Secretary of Defense to order Army, Air Force, Navy, and the Marine Corps Reserves involuntarily to active duty for a major disaster or emergency.[17] The Dual-Status Commander concept allows specifically selected and trained commanders to exercise Title 10 and Title 32 authorities concurrently. General Jacoby's testimony reinforced the evolutionary nature of homeland security operations and the whole of government approach to its provision.

Summary

The structures that comprise the homeland security organization of the United States are defined by our federal style of government. The federal style of government places numerous responsibilities on state governments to provide for the security of their citizens. Legislation enacted by Congress mandates how federal organizations interact with each other and provide services to the states. Congressional legislation illustrates United States reticence to employ federal military forces domestically for law enforcement or security operations except in special circumstances that threaten the security of the Nation. The President provides guidance and direction across the executive branch as the Chief Executive through orders and directives. The enterprise of homeland security continuously evolves in order to address threats and challenges. Sometimes these changes are anticipatory of changed circumstances, more often they are reactionary.

---

[1]U.S. Constitution.

[2]*Posse Comitatus Act*, 18 USC § 1385, http://uscode.house.gov (accessed 1 December 2011).

[3]*Insurrection Act*, 10 USC § 332, http://uscode.house.gov (accessed 1 December 2011).

[4]*Economy Act*, 31 USC § 1535, http://uscode.house.gov (accessed 1 December 2011).

[5]*Robert T. Stafford Disaster Relief and Emergency Assistance Act, as amended, and Related Authorities,* Public Law 100-707, https://www.fema.gov/library (accessed 1 December 2011).

[6]*National Security Act of 1947,* Public Law 110-53, https://www.intelligence. senate.gov/nsaact1947/pdf (accessed 13 December 2011).

[7]Paula Dobriansky, "Threats to Security in the Western Hemisphere" (Remarks at the Inter-American Defense College, Washington, DC, 20 October 2003).

[8]Vrooman, 5.

[9]U.S. President, *Presidential Decision Directive 39*, www.hsdl.org (accessed 2 December 2011).

[10]U.S. Commission on National Security/21st Century (Hart-Rudman Commission), http://www.au.af.mil/au/awc/awcgate/nssg (accessed 2 December 2011).

[11]Thomas P. M. Barnett, "The Pentagon's New Map: It Explains Why We're Going to War, and Why We'll Keep Going to War," *Esquire*, March 2003.

[12]Globalsecurity.org, "Eberhart Testimony at Confirmation Hearing, Advance Questions," http://www.globalsecurity.org/military/library/congress/2002_hr/eberhart620.pdf (accessed 15 January 2012).

[13]U.S. Department of Homeland Security, *National Strategy for Homeland Security*, October 2007, 1.

[14]Shelstad, 43.

[15]U.S. President, *Presidential Policy Directive 8*, 1, www.hsdl.org (accessed 2 December 2011).

[16]Ibid.

[17]Senate Committee on Armed Services, Statement of General Charles H. Jacoby, Jr., United States Army Commander United States Northern Command and North American Aerospace Defense Command, 113th Cong., 13 March 2012, 12-3, http://www.armed-services.senate.gov/testimony.cfm?wit_id=10401&id=5265 (accessed 26 March 2012).

CHAPTER 3

RESEARCH METHODOLOGY

Introduction

The purpose of this study was to determine if the current structure of responsibilities between DoD and DHS best achieves homeland security in a time of diminishing resources. Chapter 1 of this study provided a brief discussion of homeland security and provided the context for this study. It provided the primary research question and associated secondary research questions, as well as the limiting and delimiting factors of this study. Chapter 2 provided a literature review of the assorted strategies, policies, laws, and findings that are relevant to the exploration of the primary and secondary research questions. It provided the review organized around periods of time and the inherent challenges of our governmental design. Chapter 3 introduces and describes the research methodology that the researcher followed in order to conduct the analysis in chapter 4. Chapter 5 will provide the findings and recommendations of the study.

Methodology

In 2007, the President published his updated *National Strategy for Homeland Security* which is the current strategic document outlining the framework with which the entire Nation should conduct homeland security operations. The *National Strategy for Homeland Security, October 2007* identifies four goals with which the Nation should focus its homeland security operations: prevent and disrupt terrorist attacks; protect the American people, our critical infrastructure, and key resources; respond to and recover from incidents that do occur; and continue to strengthen the foundation to ensure our long term success.[1] Because this strategy document applies across the spectrum of the government and encapsulates the overarching goals of homeland security, it provides a useful analytical tool with which to gauge qualitative achievement of the goals of homeland security. Therefore, the researcher utilized the four goals detailed above as criteria for analysis (see figure 1).

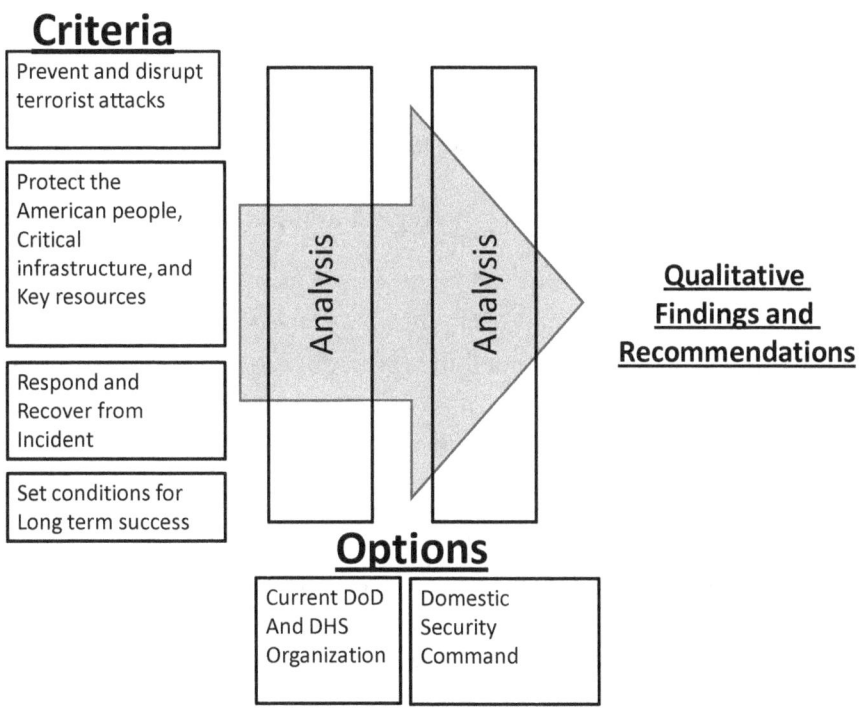

Figure 1.   Research Methodology

Source: Created by author.

A critical component of the research question is the determination of "best" with regard to the structure of responsibilities for homeland security. In order to determine best, multiple conditions, or options must be evaluated utilizing the criteria detailed above to make a determination. The researcher analyzed two options of executive federal agency design with respect to homeland security in order to determine best. The first option analyzed utilizing the four criteria was the current structures of DoD and DHS that are relevant to the homeland security. The second option the researcher analyzed is the Domestic Security Command (DSC) developed by Kristine L. Shelstad in her thesis titled, "The Domestic Security Command–The Evolution of the U.S. Northern Command." The DSC is Shelstad's recommendation of an organizational design that deconstructs and reforms elements of the DoD, DHS, and National Guard Bureau in order to better provide homeland security. The analysis of these two options provided the context and depth necessary to gauge best with regard to the current homeland security responsibilities (see figure 1).

The research question also demanded the researcher to conduct analysis with an eye towards the accomplishment of homeland security with the greatest return for the resources invested. The diminishing resources that the government has available for all its functions and responsibilities makes the relative security afforded through redundancy a luxury in the contemporary environment. Therefore, the return for investment analysis required by the research question is encapsulated in the fourth criteria: continue to strengthen the foundation to ensure our long-term success. The significance of return for investment cannot be understated in the contemporary environment of diminishing resources. Therefore, the fourth criterion achieved a status as the "first among equals" with regard to the other three criteria.

The qualitative strengths and weaknesses identified through analysis of the two options utilizing the four criteria lead the researcher to the results and findings of this study. These findings and recommendations are detailed in chapter 5 of this study which answers the research question.

Summary

Chapter 3 presented the methodology that the researcher followed to answer the primary research question and subsequent secondary research questions. Chapter 3 defined the options analyzed by the researcher utilizing the four criteria which are the goals of homeland security.

---

[1]U.S. Department of Homeland Security, *National Strategy for Homeland Security*, October 2007, 1.

CHAPTER 4

ANALYSIS

Introduction

Chapter 4 provides the analysis necessary in order to answer the purpose of this study which is to determine if the current structure of responsibilities between DoD and DHS best achieves homeland security in a time of diminishing resources. This chapter utilized the methodology introduced and described in chapter 3 which evaluates two different options for the structure of homeland security responsibilities utilizing four evaluation criteria. The analysis of these two options contains an overview of the organization (real or proposed) analyzed in order to provide a common base of reference. Following the overview, each option was analyzed utilizing the criteria: prevent and disrupt terrorist attacks; protect the American people, our critical infrastructure, and key resources; respond to and recover from incidents that do occur; and continue to strengthen the foundation to ensure our long term success. The first option analyzed was the current organization of DoD and DHS with respect to homeland security. The second option analyzed was a proposed organization where elements of the DoD, DHS, and National Guard Bureau are deconstructed and reformed into a new organization, the DSC. The hypothetical DSC formation was postulated by Kristine L. Shelstad in her thesis titled, "The Domestic Security Command–The Evolution of the U.S. Northern Command". The analysis of these two options utilizing the established criteria comprises chapter 4 and provided the basis for the recommendations and conclusion presented in chapter 5.

Option 1–Current Organization of DoD and DHS

Overview

The DoD and DHS are the principle entities responsible for homeland security at the federal level. The *Homeland Security Act of 2002* and *Homeland Security Presidential Directive 5* identified the Secretary of DHS as the principle federal official responsible for the management of all homeland security activities.[1] The DoD is primarily in a supporting role to DHS when conducting homeland security activities. The primary DoD agent for homeland security operations and support is USNORTHCOM, the GCC responsible for the all the territorial land mass of the United States and her territories, Canada, Mexico, as well as the coastal waters extending up to 500 nautical miles from shore. While USNORTHCOM is the primary provider of civil support operations, there are elements of other GCCs that can play a role in homeland security. USNORTHCOM provides civil support to DHS through DSCA operations.

DHS is comprised of over 240,000 personnel with wide ranging and diverse responsibilities.[2] DHS is lead by the Secretary of Homeland Security, a member of the president's cabinet. DHS was formed on 1 March 2003 as a result of the *Homeland Security Act of 2002* and merged over 22 federal agencies and programs under the DHS umbrella. The overall mission of DHS is to enact "a concerted national effort to ensure a homeland that is safe, secure, and resilient against terrorism and other hazards where American interests, aspirations, and way of life can thrive:"[3] This wide ranging and expansive mission gives DHS broad responsibilities and numerous functions across the federal government. In order to accomplish these responsibilities, DHS has established three directorates which conduct administrative and coordination activities across the width and depth of the nation's governmental and civilian sectors: Management; National Protection and Programs, and Science and Technology. DHS utilizes seven operational components to implement programs, policies, and perform homeland security duties across the nation. The operational components are the Transportation Security Administration, U.S. Customs and Border Protection, U.S. Citizenship and Immigration Services, U.S. Immigration and Customs Enforcement, Secret Service, Federal Emergency Management Agency (FEMA), and the United States Coast Guard.[4] In addition to the numerous federal agencies DHS is responsible for and coordinates with, they interface with all 50 state governments and over 87,000 different local jurisdictions.[5] The mandate for DHS is all encompassing and wide ranging from the federal to the local level.

DoD provides numerous liaisons and representatives throughout the DHS. DoD also provides representatives to the Joint Field Office, which is the primary federal incident response organization. Additionally, there is a Defense Coordinating Officer at each of the ten FEMA regions. The Defense Coordinating Officer is the single point of contact for the Joint Field Office when DoD support is requested. Additionally, a Joint Task Force commander is usually assigned from the DoD, based upon the level of DoD support when responding to a domestic incident. The Joint Task Force commander, when assigned, reports to the Joint Field Office

USNORTHCOM is commanded by a military four star general who reports directly to Secretary of Defense, a member of the president's cabinet. There are currently over 2,000 personnel permanently assigned to USNORTHCOM. They perform planning and coordination operations in the headquarters and staffs of USNORTHCOM, there are no military formations permanently assigned to USNORTHCOM. Military forces and capabilities are assigned to USNORTHCOM on an as needed basis based upon mission requirements by the Secretary of Defense. Approximately 1200 of the permanently assigned military personnel to USNORTHCOM are assigned to the USNORTHCOM headquarters. The remainder of the permanently assigned military personnel are assigned to its four service component commands, three standing joint task forces, and one joint force headquarters. Approximately 60 percent of the USNORTHCOM headquarters is military, 15 percent of which is comprised of National Guard personnel to include the USNORTHCOM deputy commander as mandated by the National Defense Authorization Act of 2008. There are also approximately 60 interagency personnel in the USNORTHCOM headquarters representing over 40 non-DoD federal organizations which include personnel from DHS.

Throughout DoD there are numerous interfaces with DHS. Following the attacks of 11 September 2001 and in line with recommendations from the Hart-Rudman Commission, the DoD created an Assistant Secretary for Homeland Defense who is the prime linkage between DoD and DHS in order to coordinate the overlapping intergovernmental operations between DoD and DHS necessary to perform homeland security operations. At the GCC level, USNORTHCOM has numerous personnel on its staff representing the interests of DHS. These personnel include a DHS Senior Executive Service (one star general equivalent) advisor to the USNORTHCOM commander as well as over twenty U.S. Coast Guard officers on the USNORTHCOM staff.

DHS is the lead federal agency for homeland security. DoD provides support to DHS in accordance with applicable laws and regulations. USNORTHCOM is the primary element of DoD that directly partners with DHS to conduct homeland security through DSCA operations to defend and secure the United States.[6]

Prevent and Disrupt Terrorist Attacks

It can be reasonably argued that the preponderance of the DoD's actions to achieve this criterion are conducted by the GCCs other than USNORTHCOM through their overseas operations as part of anti-terrorism operations. USNORTHCOM is specifically prevented from conducting offensive operations to prevent and disrupt attacks within the United States by the *10th Amendment* and the *Posse Comitatus Act*. The only exception to these restrictions would be in the event of extraordinary circumstances, whereby the DoD would take the lead to protect and defend the people and territory of the United States with other federal agencies in support. This authorization would have to be received from the President, exercising his enumerated powers as the Commander in Chief and the Chief Executive.[7]

The operations of USNORTHCOM are also a matter of concern for governors during emergency and non-emergency circumstances. Emergency circumstances occur after a terrorist attack, disaster, or other catastrophe that requires military capabilities or when other agencies have been overwhelmed while non-emergency situations are limited in duration and scope and are generally planned events. Governors have expressed concerns regarding state sovereignty resulting from potential violation of the *10th Amendment* when active duty troops are deployed within state boundaries under these circumstances. A potential solution to this is the utilization of National Guard forces when unique capabilities are required that are not inherent to state and local governments. Unfortunately, USNORTHCOM cannot exercise command and control of National

Guard troops that have not been transferred to Title 10 authority. Therefore, USNORTHCOM has no legal authorization to prevent or disrupt terrorist attacks during emergency and non-emergency circumstances. The lack of legal authorization has been identified by the Constitution Project which registered concerns that USNORTHCOM would not be able to operate within the federalist legal framework while accomplishing their mission.[8]

The ability of DHS to prevent and disrupt terrorist attacks within the United States exceeds the abilities and authorization of DoD under Title 10 authorizations. DHS, being a civilian entity is not subject to the restrictions placed upon the DoD by the *Posse Comitatus Act*. Therefore, the operational elements of the DHS can and do conduct domestic law enforcement operations. The Coast Guard, while technically a member of the Armed Forces, was imbued by Congress with law enforcement authority.[9] Therefore, one can reasonably argue that all the operational elements of DHS are primarily law enforcement entities. DoD is limited to a support role and does not have the "assigned responsibility to stop terrorists from coming across our borders"[10] The DoD does have authorization to conduct support operations as well as counterterrorism operations when lead by other government agencies.[11] It is clearly articulated that DoD Title 10 personnel are in a dedicated support role when conducting counterterrorism operations within the United States.

Protect American People, Critical Infrastructure,
and Key Resources

One of the most important areas in which DHS has freedom to operate is in the collection and analysis of intelligence. Intelligence is commonly believed to be the "first line of defense for the nation"[12] and is therefore essential in order to achieve the criterion of protecting the American people, critical infrastructure, and key resources. The DHS Under Secretary for Intelligence and Analysis is the primary intelligence officer for DHS. Unencumbered by legal restrictions as a result of the *Homeland Security Act of 2002* and subsequent legislation enacted based upon recommendations of the 9-11 Commission,[13] the Under Secretary is able to consult on a daily basis with all the elements of US foreign intelligence as well as local, state, and private sector intelligence collectors and agencies in order to develop homeland security intelligence (see figure 2).

The use of the term "homeland security intelligence" is not well defined by law but is important to understand because it provides linkages between the separate and disparate sources of intelligence. The ability to collaborate and coordinate between all the members of the intelligence community is a key capability of DHS.

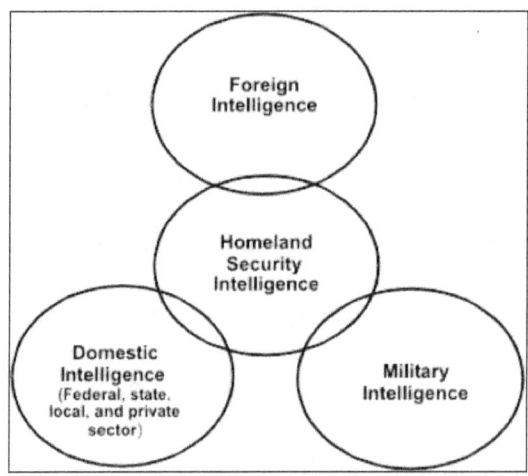

Figure 2.   Dimensions of Intelligence

Source: Mark A. Randol, *Homeland Security Intelligence: Perceptions, Statutory Definitions, and Approaches* (Washington, DC: Congressional Research Service, 14 January 2009), http://www.fas.org/sgp/crs/index.html (accessed 28 March 2012), 6.

The National Guard provides critical capabilities and resources to homeland security operations. The capabilities and resources provided by the National Guard thread a fine legal line as their Title 32 operations are not constrained by *Posse Comitatus Act*. Additionally, Title 32 status can be maintained when their pay and benefits are provided by the Federal government contingent upon their operations being conducted under the control of their state governor(s). Because of the capabilities of Title 32 forces, the *Beyond Goldwater Nichols Phase II Report* recommended that the National Guard should form regional civil support teams to be employed in accordance with the DoD force management and rotation plans in order to enhance the National Guard's homeland security capabilities.[14] Unfortunately, USNORTHCOM has no legal standing or authorization to coordinate or compel the National Guard to form regional teams. Only the National Guard Bureau has the authority to mandate the formation of the aforementioned regional teams.

USNORTHCOM conducts planning and exercises with the intent of increasing their capability to achieve this criterion. USNORTHCOM relies upon the State Adjutant Generals, the senior National Guard Officers of each state, to be the unofficial conduit of information to their respective state and local governments. USNORTHCOM has to rely upon this informal method of information exchange because they do not have the formal authority necessary to facilitate collaboration with state and local entities.[15] The result is that planning and coordination conducted by USNORTHCOM is not synchronized across the applicable levels of government which will likely result in critical delays and a lack of unity of effort in the event that Title 10 forces are employed in a homeland security scenario.

USNORTHCOM is a GCC with responsibilities for homeland security through DSCA missions, as well as the more traditional homeland defense role. U.S. Government Accountability Office (GAO) reports from 2008 criticized USNORTHCOM for focusing on the homeland defense roles as a GCC while giving short shrift to the more likely DSCA mission. This lack of focus on the DSCA mission, coupled with the lack of synchronization with state and local governments raises questions about USNORTHCOM's ability to effectively support homeland security operations.

Respond and Recover from Incident

The *National Response Framework* outlines how the Nation conducts all-hazards response following a homeland security incident. It is built upon five principles: engaged partnerships; tiered response; scalable, flexible and adaptable operational capabilities; unity of effort through unified command; and readiness to act. It details and describes how all levels of government and private sector partners respond to an incident in order to achieve an effective national response. The DHS Secretary is the "principal Federal official responsible for domestic incident management"[16] while the FEMA Administrator is the principle advisor to the DHS Secretary for emergency management. The *National Response Framework* also identifies lead agencies, referred to as Emergency Support Function Coordinators who are responsible for the coordination of all governmental and non-governmental support agencies.

> The ESF[Emergency Support Function]s serve as the primary operational-level mechanism to provide assistance in functional areas such as transportation, communications, public works and engineering, firefighting, mass care, housing, human services, public health and medical services, search and rescue, agriculture and natural resources, and energy.[17]

36

It is important to note that the DoD, specifically the U.S. Army Corps of

Engineers, is the Emergency Support Function Coordinator for only one of the fifteen

functional areas: Emergency Support Function #3-public works and engineering. Based

upon the responsibilities of the DoD identified in the *National Response Framework*,

DoD and USNORTHCOM can expect to only be called upon in response to an incident

in a supporting role when other agencies have been overwhelmed or are no longer

capable of performing their necessary functions with the exception of Emergency

Support Function #3.

> In providing civil support, USNORTHCOM generally operates through
> established Joint Task Forces subordinate to the command. An emergency must
> exceed the capabilities of local, state and federal agencies before
> USNORTHCOM becomes involved. In most cases, support will be limited,
> localized and specific. When the scope of the disaster is reduced to the point that
> the Primary Agency can again assume full control and management without
> military assistance, USNORTHCOM will exit, leaving the on-scene experts to
> finish the job.[18]

Numerous reports have found that DoD, and USNORTHCOM in particular are

unprepared to execute their responsibilities within the *National Response Framework*.

GAO Report 08-252 identified gaps in coordination between USNORTHCOM, state

governments, and the National Guard. USNORTHCOM did not involve the majority of

the states when they developed homeland defense and civil support plans as less than 25

percent of the states were involved in the development of USNORTHCOM plans.

Additionally, USNORTHCOM is not familiar with and has no mechanism for the access

of state level response plans as there are no established processes at USNORTHCOM for

interfacing with state governments. These gaps are inconsistent with *Homeland Security*

Presidential Directive 8 which called for plans and actions to be synchronized and deconflicted between the federal, state, and local levels as well as the requirements delineated in the *National Response Framework*.[19]

A critical capability provided by DoD to DHS is their expertise in the response to Chemical, Biological, Radiological, Nuclear, and High-Explosive (CBRNE) events. This does not mean that DoD will be the first responders in the event of a CBRNE incident, but rather they provide expertise, capabilities, equipment, and manpower. GAO Report 10-123 also found that DoD support elements tasked to provide expertise, capabilities and equipment in the event of a CBRNE incident are not synchronized between the active and reserve components. Additionally, agreements between the National Guard units and the active component for the availability of National Guard units was not complete putting into question the DoD's ability to train and deploy appropriate forces in response to a CBRNE event because of equipment, personnel, and capability shortfalls.[20]

Two Congressional reports in 2008 found that USNORTHCOM lacks the ability to adequately plan, support, assess readiness, and coordinate with state and local officials. The reports contend that USNORTHCOM has not evolved into an integrated command capable of emergency preparedness or response.[21] While USNORTHCOM organizational structures utilize integrated staffing in order to bridge the gap and facilitate communication between themselves, National Guard, and DHS it does little to integrate at the State and local levels because of a lack of authority.

Set Conditions for Long Term Success

DHS completed its first ever *Quadrennial Homeland Security Review* as well as a *Bottom Up Review* in 2010. The underlying themes of these two reviews was that while much has been accomplished by the nascent DHS, there is still room for improvement in order to provide homeland security to the United States. The *Bottom Up Review* demonstrates a maturity on the part of the department as well as the realization that they must be better stewards of the finite resources of the government in order to accomplish their mandate. The DHS budget for 2012 was $59.7 billion dollars with a decrease of 0.5 percent for 2013 to $59.0 billion dollars.[22] The *Bottom Up Review* identified areas where increased efficiencies will be utilized and sought in order to make up the contracting budget without impacting accomplishment of their mission effectiveness.

DoD budget is decreasing from $645 billion in 2012 to a request of $613 billion in 2013, a reduction of 31.8 billion or 0.5 percent. There is also the expectation that the DoD budget will continue to remain at roughly the 2013 level through 2017 in order to achieve a total projected savings of $259.4 billion.[23] As with DHS, DoD is seeking to increase efficiencies while also delaying major procurement items in order to operate within their budget without negatively affecting their mission effectiveness.

While DoD is striving to maintain existing mission effectiveness with decreased budgetary resources, recent findings by the GAO showed problems with the provision of resources to fulfill critical CBRNE capabilities within DoD. GAO identified the inability of a central funding accountability manager within the DoD between the active and national guard forces tasked with responding to CBRNE events as detrimental to the long term viability of CBRNE capability. The lack of a central funding manager calls into question the ability of the DoD to identify all requirements and allocate funding and resources appropriately.[24] In order to address these shortfalls, USNORTHCOM expect the newly created CBRNE Response Enterprise which includes National Guard, Reserve, and Active Component forces to achieve full operational readiness by October 2012.

These 18,000 Soldiers assigned to the mission will be prepared to" rapidly respond to a

CBRN incident within the homeland."[25]

In order to address the limitations imposed by the restrictions associated with

Title 10 and Title 32 constraints on the National Guard, USNORTHCOM has instituted

and certified the Dual-Status Commander Concept but actual implementation has been

limited to only forecasted events.

> USNORTHCOM led the development and implementation of the Dual-Status
> Commander Concept of Operations. This has allowed the DoD and the State
> governors to jointly pre-identify, train, and certify senior military officers to
> perform simultaneously as commanders of both National Guard forces in State
> status and Federal military forces in Title 10 status.[26]

The development of the Dual-Status Commander Concept as well as the CBRNE

Response Enterprise is a clear indication that DoD, and USNORTHCOM in particular are

making proactive changes to rectify areas of weakness within their ability to perform

civil support as required in their mission statement.

Option 2–The Domestic Security Command (DSC)

Overview of the Organization

In her 2011 thesis presented to the Naval Postgraduate School, Kristine L.

Shelstad developed a model for the formation of the DSC to perform the most likely

homeland security and defense scenarios utilizing civilian interagency team while being

able to address the most dangerous scenarios through its organic military-led teams. The

DSC, as envisioned by Shelstad, involves the deconstruction of USNORTHCOM,

selected elements of other GCCs, DHS, and the National Guard Bureau Joint Staff and

the use of their applicable parts to create the DSC as a federal agency focused on

decentralized homeland security and defense operations. In addition to the amalgamation of these disparate elements into the DSC, the DSC will incorporate planning elements from other federal agencies such as the Department of Health and Human Services, Department of Justice, and the Department of Energy in order to achieve intergovernmental coordination.

The DSC will conduct operations in a decentralized manner, with increasing levels of the organization becoming involved as situations or events increase in scope and/or severity. The lowest level will be the state response orchestrated by the state governor utilizing the state and local resources at his disposal, including their state National Guard formations. The state would form a Joint Task Force utilizing a dual status commander in order to respond to the situation.

If the situation requires more resources or expertise than the state level Joint Task Force provides or encompasses more than one state the regional hub will provide resources and take control of the response in a federal manner. These regional hubs will be based upon the existing FEMA districts, which divide the United States into ten different regions. The regional hubs will have all of the current equity holders from the DHS organization as well as the DoD and National Guard Bureau equities resident in the region. The DoD equities in the region will be represented by the Defense Coordinating Officer, a similar position to today's FEMA construct, while National Guard Bureau equities will be represented through a Homeland Response Force. The Homeland Response Force are National Guard forces with focused expertise in CBRNE. The regional DHS hub would spawn an inherently interagency team to augment the state Joint Task Force. Additionally, the regional hub would be responsible for conducting contingency planning and normal operations for their region.

41

At the national level, the DSC will be interagency and intergovernmental through the merging of the DHS, National Guard Bureau, and DoD entities with equities. A national level DSC response to an incident would occur when an incident involves multiple regions, is homeland defense oriented, or is exceedingly damaging and overwhelms the regional capacity. National level DSC response would be conducted through the provision of interagency capabilities to augment the regional center's response as well as coordinating the resources and responses from other regional hubs. Through the implementation of state, regional, and national structures the DSC would be able to provide decentralized homeland defense and homeland security capabilities.

The DSC is envisioned as a civilian led organization whose secretary is independent of the governmental agencies from which it was formed. The DSC Secretary will be supported by deputy commanders from the National Guard, Title 10 active component, DHS deputy, a Domestic Advisor, and a Political Advisor. The National Guard deputy serves as the conduit between the states Adjutant General and represents their interests in the DSC. The Title 10 active component deputy will coordinate the situational awareness and planning activities undertaken by the Defense Coordination Officers at the ten regional hubs as well as being responsible for traditional security cooperation activities with Canada and Mexico. The DHS deputy represents all the organizations that comprise the current DHS as well as the prime coordinator with law enforcement agencies. The Domestic Advisor represents the Council of Governors and their resident equities in state and local organizations. The Political Advisor is drawn from the Department of State and provides the expertise and advice to the DSC Commander with regard to relations with Mexico and Canada (see figure 3).

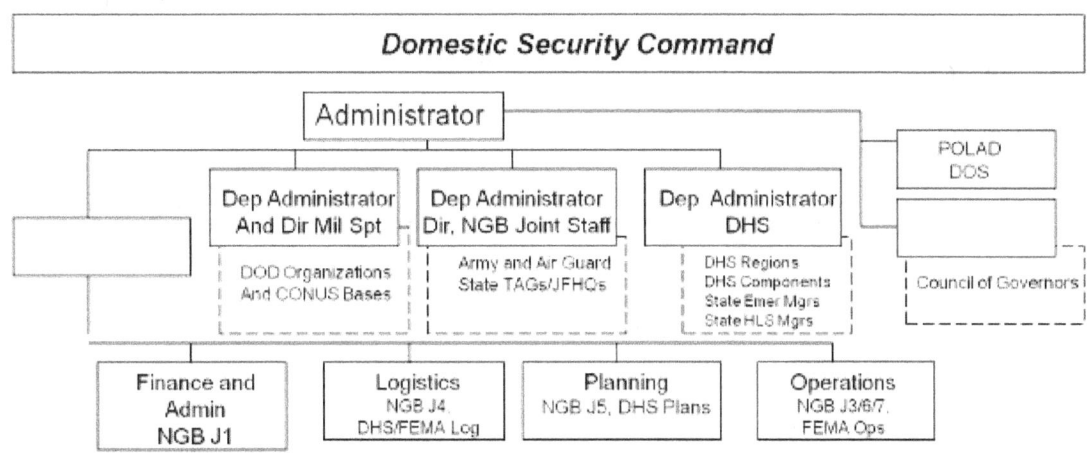

Figure 3.   Domestic Security Command

Source: Kristine L. Shelstad, "The Domestic Security Command–The Evolution of the U.S. Northern Command" (Master's Thesis, Naval Postgraduate School, Monterrey, CA, 2011), 47.

Prevent and Disrupt Terrorist Attacks

The DSC design, as detailed, has impacts upon the Unified Command Plan, the

order that the President signs to delineate the GCC's. The deconstruction of

USNORTHCOM to form critical elements of the DSC responsible for homeland defense

and homeland security effectively ends its applicability as well as the dual responsibilities

of the commander with regard to USNORTHCOM and NORAD. While not directly

addressed by the DSC concept, it is reasonable to expect that NORAD would revert to an

independent command under the DoD as it was prior to the establishment of

USNORTHCOM. The DSC concept also calls for the elements currently assigned to

Pacific Command and Southern Command that provide resources to conduct civil support

operations to be moved under the control of the DSC. The transfer of these units and

resources would require presidential authorization. Operations conducted by other GCC's under the auspices of anti-terrorism would be unaffected by the deconstruction of USNORTHCOM.

The DSC organizational concept directly addresses the concerns of state sovereignty expressed by state governors and independent researchers such as the Constitution Project. The DSC places Title 32 National Guard commanders in the chain of command. The Dual-Status Commander Concept allows properly screened and vetted Title 10 active component senior leaders to exercise mission command over National Guard troops operating under Title 32 authorities. The provision of the Title 32 and Dual-Status Commanders effectively addresses the federalist concerns of state governors and negates sovereignty arguments as all commanders are responsive to the intent of state governors.

The DSC has the ability to conduct domestic law enforcement operations through the incorporation of DHS elements as well as National Guard elements without any changes or modifications to existing policies or legislation. While Title 10 active forces have the capability to perform law enforcement operations, they must be specifically authorized by Congress or the President in accordance with applicable legislation and Constitutional authority. It is important to remember that Title 10 forces will not be routinely assigned to the DSC, but rather to the Joint Task Forces established by state or regional DSC headquarters based upon direction of the President and/or the Secretary of Defense.

Protect American People, Critical Infrastructure, and Key Resources

The ability to conduct intelligence is a critical capability necessary to achieve this criterion. The DSC has the ability and legal justification to conduct domestic intelligence collection through the integration of the operational elements of DHS. The DSC also includes intergovernmental ties and linkages to domestic law enforcement agencies through the federal level organization as well as the regional centers that can result in increased intelligence sharing. The failures in intelligence sharing were identified as one of the key factors leading to the attacks of 11 September 2001. The perceptions identified by the Constitution Project of the militarization of society through the perceived spying by military forces within the United States are also avoided.

The National Guard is directly tied into the DSC and therefore can be fully employed and utilized by the DSC. The utilization of the National Guard deputy DSC commander connects the state Adjutant Generals directly to the DSC. Thereby, the unique capabilities of the national guard to conduct operations within the United States is harnessed and coordinated directly to work toward homeland security operations. Additionally, the linkage between the DSC and the Adjutant Generals can lead directly to the integration of unique military capabilities to the state and local governments. This authority to conduct direct communications, as well as the infrastructure provided by the regional hubs provides for a more integrated and synchronized response between the numerous equity holders.

The lack of GCC type responsibilities allows for the DSC, the Title 10 deputy specifically, to focus on the core competencies of homeland defense without giving short shrift to the responsibilities of homeland security. The Title 10 deputy therefore can focus

45

his staff on the planning necessary to establish a Joint Task Force as required to respond to the most dangerous, but least likely scenario, of protecting the homeland from invasion and military attack. In this capacity, the Title 10 deputy will accomplish many of the requirements that were formerly performed by USNORTHCOM. Additionally, the potential for the Title 10 deputy to receive Dual Status authority provides for the ability to leverage the National Guard as part of his operations without previous authorization from the President or Congress in response to emerging events. Additionally, the collaboration between the National Guard deputy and Title 10 deputy can be reasonably expected to reduce turbulence and lower the learning curve when operations change. This increased interoperability between the National Guard and the active force will result in increased effectiveness and the ability to transition between homeland security and homeland defense roles and responsibilities.

Respond and Recover from Incident

The *National Response Framework* would not be negatively affected by the establishment of the DSC as it was intended to form the conceptual model for a whole of nation response to respond and recover from an incident. Other than title changes to reflect the transfer of responsibilities from DHS to DSC, there are few mandatory changes required in order to maintain its integrity. The DSC outline did not address any recommended changes to the organization of the Army Corps of Engineers, who are responsible to be the lead agency for Emergency Support Function 3. The allocation of the Corps of Engineers into the design of the DSC appears to be a value added addition in order to increase the interagency capabilities of the DSC and take advantage of the unique organizational structure of the active, national guard, and civilian personnel that comprise the Corps of Engineers.

The construct of the DSC removes the inherent conflicts between homeland defense and homeland security operations for active military forces. In order for the DSC to conduct homeland defense operations with active forces it would require the assigning of forces by the Secretary of Defense. Active forces would not be routinely assigned, except for the provision of standing Joint Task Forces. National Guard units will be able to focus on homeland security type operations while still being synchronized from the state to federal levels.

The expansion of the Defense Coordinating Officer at the regional hubs as envisioned under the DSC provides increased interoperability and intergovernmental communications. The Defense Coordinating Officers will have the ability to incorporate any active forces into the existing state and local response plans and activities. This increased ability and authorization to conduct liaison activities to the lowest level alleviates many of the failings demonstrated through the operations of USNORTHCOM.

Set Conditions for Long Term Success

The establishment of the DSC would result in an immense restructuring of the federal government. It would amalgamate elements of DHS, DoD, and the National Guard Bureau into one organization. All three of these organizations have different streams of funding and resourcing which would significantly complicate the budgeting and resourcing operations. Besides resourcing issues, there would be significant cultural challenges faced in the creation of the DSC. The organization structures and functions of these disparate entities would lead to significant turbulence which has the potential to compromise the short term effectiveness of the organization.

While it is outside the scope of this study to make resource projections, it is safe to assume that the establishment of the DSC would require a large obligation of governmental resources. These resources would be required at the federal level as the federal organization is staffed and headquartered. While the resources obligated are sufficient to sustain operations as currently organized, the establishment of a new headquarters and associated staff would be a significant investment. It is also reasonable to expect that additional resources would be required at the state and local level in order to incorporate their plans and activities with the emergent DSC.

One of the advantages of the DSC is that it is designed to conduct operations in a decentralized manner. The advantages of decentralized operations are that they are inherently more responsive and tailored to the situations they address. The increased responsiveness and tailoring of operations results in a more focused application of resources to address the needs of homeland security and defense in the local and state environments.

While decentralized operation are inherently more responsive and tailored, they can also be overly redundant. The establishment of the DSC calls for the expansion of the ten current FEMA regions to become DSC hubs with increased presence from all the component and operational organizations inherent in DHS as well as the National Guard and element of the DoD. The establishment of these ten regional hubs can be reasonably expected to result in the duplication of capabilities and negate the advantages of efficiencies of scale offered by centralized operations. Therefore, the resources required to staff and operate ten regional hubs would be an increase from the current organization of DHS and DoD.

Summary

The analysis presented in chapter 4 provides the rationale and background information necessary to inform the recommendations and conclusions that encapsulated in chapter 5. The analysis of the current organization of DoD and DHS with respect to homeland security provides the baseline of performance. The identification and construction of the hypothetical DSC, and subsequent analysis provides a well developed alternative to judge against the current organization of DoD and DHS. While the qualitative analysis of a topic as broad and expansive as homeland security and the relationship between DHS and DoD is daunting, the elements presented in chapter 4 provide clear insight into the ability of the government to provide homeland security in a time of diminishing resources.

---

[1]U.S. Department of Homeland Security, *National Response Framework* (Washington, DC: Government Printing Office, January 2008), http://www. fema.gov/emergency/nrf/ (accessed 21 March 2012), 6.

[2]U.S. Department of Homeland Security, *Fiscal Year 2012 Budget Request–U.S. Department of Homeland Security(Overview)* (Washington DC: Government Printing Office, 2012), http://www.dhs.gov/xabout/budget/dhs-budget.shtm (accessed 28 March 2012).

[3]U.S. Department of Homeland Security, *Quadrennial Homeland Security Review Report: A Strategic Framework for a Secure Homeland* (Washington, DC: Government Printing Office, February 2010), http://www.dhs.gov/xabout/gc_1208534155450.shtm#0 (accessed 28 March 2012), 13.

[4]U.S. Department of Homeland Security, *Homeland Security Organizational Chart.*

[5]U.S. Department of Homeland Security, *National Strategy for Homeland Security*, July 2002, 11.

[6]USNORTHCOM.mil, http://www.northcom.mil/About/index.html (accessed 27 March 2012).

[7]U.S. Department of Defense, *The DoD Role in Homeland Security–Defense Study and Report To Congress* (Washington, DC: Government Printing Office, July 2003), www.ndu.edu/uchs/ (accessed 28 March 2012), 2.

[8]Constitution Project, *Potential Constitutional, Legal and Policy Issues Raised by a Unified Command for the Domestic United States: An Interim Report of the Constitution Project*, 2-3, http://www.constitutionproject.org/ pdf/Northcom_Interim.pdf (accessed 27 March 2012).

[9]R. Chuck Mason, *Securing America's Borders: The Role of the Military,* (Washington, DC: Congressional Research Service, 16 June 2010), http://www.fas.org/ sgp/crs/index.html (accessed 28 March 2012), 4.

[10]U.S. Department of Defense, *Strategy for Homeland Defense and Civil Support* (Washington, DC: Government Printing Office, June 2005), http://www.defense.gov/ news/Jun2005/d20050630homeland.pdf (accessed 28 March 2012).

[11]Mason, 1.

[12]Mark A. Randol, *Homeland Security Intelligence: Perceptions, Statutory Definitions, and Approaches* (Washington, DC: Congressional Research Service, 14 January 2009), 6, http://www.fas.org/sgp/crs/index.html (accessed 28 March 2012).

[13]Randol, 8.

[14]Clark Murdock, Pierre Chao, Anne A. Witkowsky, Michele A. Flournoy, and Christine E. Wormuth, Mac Bollman, Jeremiah Gertler, Adam N. Marks, Noah J. Richmond, David R. Scruggs, and Richard Weitz, *Beyond Goldwater-Nichols: U.S. Government and Defense Reform for a New Strategic Era–Phase 2 Report* (Washington, DC: Center for Strategic and International Studies, July 2005), 9, http://csis.org/publication/beyond-goldwater-nichols-phase-ii-report (accessed 27 March 2012).

[15]Shelstad, 26.

[16]U.S. Department of Homeland Security, *National Response Framework* (Washington, DC: Government Printing Office, January 2008), 54, http://www.fema. gov/emergency/nrf/ (accessed 21 March 2012).

[17]U.S. Department of Homeland Security, *National Response Framework*, 57.

[18]USNORTHCOM.mil.

[19]U.S. Government Accountability Office, GAO Report 08-252, *Homeland Defense–Steps Have Been Taken to Improve U.S. Northern Command's Coordination with States and the National Guard Bureau, but Gaps Remain* (Washington, DC: Government Printing Office, April 2008), http://www.gao.gov (accessed 15 March 2012), 2.

[20]U.S. Government Accountability Office, GAO Report 10-123, *Homeland Defense–Planning, Resourcing, and Training Issue Challenge DoD's Response to Domestic Chemical, Biological, Radiological, Nuclear, and High-Yield Explosive Incidents* (Washington, DC: Government Printing Office, October 2009), http://www.gao.gov (accessed 15 March 2012), 2.

[21]U.S. Government Accountability Office, GAO Report 08-252, 2.

[22]U.S. Department of Homeland Security, *FY13 Budget in Brief* (Washington, DC: Government Printing Office, 2012), 3, http://www.dhs.gov/xabout/budget/dhs-budget.shtm (accessed 28 March 2012).

[23]U.S. Department of Defense, *Fiscal Year 2013 Budget Request* (Washington DC, February 2012), 1-1 to 1-3, http://comptroller.defense.gov/ budget2013.html (accessed 29 March 2012).

[24]U.S. Government Accountability Office, GAO Report 10-123, 2.

[25]Senate Committee on Armed Services, 12.

[26]Ibid., 13.

CHAPTER 5

CONCLUSION AND RECOMMENDATIONS

Introduction

Chapter 5 provides the outputs of this study which endeavored to determine if the current organization of DoD and DHS best achieves homeland security in a time of diminishing resources. These outputs are in the form of a conclusion and associated recommendations. The conclusion and associated recommendations are based on and supported by the analysis performed in chapter 4 through the application of the research methodology outlined in chapter 3.

Conclusion

In the immediate aftermath of the attacks of 11 September 2001 the Federal Government pursued rational and expected actions to determine what happened, who was responsible, and how to improve homeland security in order to prevent future attacks and manage effects should prevention fail. Congress passed significant legislation, the *Homeland Security Act of 2002*, which resulted in the formation of the DHS through the amalgamation of 22 assorted federal entities. The formation of DHS resulted in the second largest federal organization, second to only the DoD, in terms of fiscal allocations and personnel size. The President established USNORTHCOM as a GCC acting in his role as the Commander-in-Chief in order to achieve unity of effort within the DoD for the provision of homeland defense, homeland security, and civil support operations.

The creation of DHS and changes to DoD structure in the aftermath of 11 September 2001 resulted in the overdue updating of United States Cold War homeland security institutions, keeping with the findings of the Hart-Rudman Commission. These changes enhanced the United States' homeland security. While these changes have served the United States well, they are not without fault or room for improvement.

The primary research question of this study was to determine if the current organization of DoD and DHS best achieves homeland security in a time of diminishing resources. The secondary research questions of the study were: what are the DoD responsibilities and obligations for homeland security, what functions does DHS perform to ensure homeland security, and what responsibilities are held at the state level with regard to homeland security. To answer these questions, the current DoD and DHS organization was analyzed vice the DSC utilizing criterion derived from the goals of the *National Strategy for Homeland Defense*. By comparing the current organization to a notional alternative organization, the researcher sought determine if a better alternative exists to the current DoD and DHS organization. This comparison answered the primary research question by offering a superior alternative to the current organization. The determination of the best organization for homeland security was outside the scope of this research.

The first criterion for analysis was the organizational ability to prevent and disrupt terrorist attacks. Analysis demonstrated that there are significant restrictions on the current organization because of the constraints of our federalist system and various laws that restrict the operations of DoD. These restrictions do not exist in the DSC organization as it was specifically designed to alleviate the federalist and legal constraints. Therefore, the DSC organization was a better option to prevent and disrupt terrorist attacks (see figure 4).

The second criterion for analysis was the organizational ability to protect the American people, critical infrastructure, and key resources. Analysis demonstrated that the lack of authority for USNORTHCOM, the DoD principal agent for civil support, to direct the organization and operations of the National Guard is a critical shortcoming of the current organization. The current organization also benefits from the lack of legal definition and restriction from the gathering of homeland security intelligence. The DSC organization addresses the lack of USNORTHCOM control over the National Guard through the deconstruction and amalgamation of select parts of these organizations. Therefore, the DSC organization was a better option to protect the American people, critical infrastructure, and key resources (see figure 4).

The third criterion for analysis was the organizational ability to respond and recover from an incident should one occur. Analysis demonstrated that the lack of authority for USNORTHCOM to conduct contingency coordination and planning meetings with state agencies prior to an event was a significant shortcoming. The DSC does not suffer from this lack of authority and possessed a robust ability to conduct decentralized contingency planning and rehearsals with state agencies. Therefore, the DSC organization was a better option to respond and recover from an incident should one occur (see figure 4).

The fourth criterion for analysis was whether the organization set conditions for long term success. As detailed in chapter 3, this criterion was the first among equals because the significance of return for investment cannot be overstated in the current environment of diminishing resources. The recent and ongoing experiments with the training and certification of Dual-Status Commanders by USNORTHCOM has the capability to address and overcome the many limitations imposed by legislation and our

federalist governmental design with respect to domestic utilization of Title 10 forces.

Additionally, the current organization is accomplishing the mission of providing

homeland security while simultaneously reducing their budgetary requirements. The

establishment of the DSC would require immense government restructuring and

budgeting of the two largest executive agencies. The resources required to affect this

restructuring are inconsistent with diminishing resources in the short term. An

assumption for this study was that one organization will be inherently more efficient than

two organizations to exercise the same responsibilities. Therefore, in the long term the

creation of the DSC is consistent with diminishing resources. Therefore, the DSC

organization was a better option to set the conditions for long term success (see figure 4).

	Current DoD and DHS Organization	Domestic Security Command (DSC)
Prevent and Disrupt Terrorist Attacks		BEST
Protect the American People, Critical Infrastructure, and Key Resources		BEST
Respond and Recover from Incident		BEST
Set Conditions for Long Term Success		BEST

Figure 4.   Analysis Chart

Source: Created by author.

Finding

The current organization of DoD and DHS does not best achieve homeland security in a time of diminishing resources.

Recommendations

The current tests and limited implementation of Dual-Status Commander authority conducted by USNORTHCOM should be refined and expanded to include emergency and non-emergency situations. The Dual-Status Commander provides a key capability within the DoD to conduct DSCA operations without impinging upon state sovereignty or exceeding limitations on the domestic use of federal military forces. The ability of a Dual-Status commander to serve as a JTF Commander for civil support operations for emergency and non-emergency operations is a capability that needs to be incorporated into contingency operations planning and execution. The ongoing tests by USNORTHCOM with Dual-Status Commander authority has the potential to fundamentally alter the findings of this study.

Additional research should be conducted that performs a cost benefit analysis of USNORTHCOM. The limitations imposed upon the command by the federalist model of government and congressional legislation severely limit the applicability of USNORTHCOM to conduct operations as a GCC within the domestic environment. The only exception to these limitations is in response or anticipation of a military attack upon the United States or an insurrection as determined by the president. It is not clear if the structure, authority, and capabilities of a GCC are required in order to satisfactorily remedy a direct attack or the threat posed by an insurrection. The benefits of

USNORTHCOM may not be commensurate with the resources it requires in order to conduct its current operations.

Additional research into the applicability and feasibility of the creation of a standing JTF headquarters commanded by a Dual-Status Commander and organizationally linked to DHS should be conducted. This standing JTF could form the command structure for civil support operations as well as be provide the planning and coordination with the state adjutant generals for the nesting of federal and state emergency response plans. Additionally, this standing JTF headquarters could potentially assume the homeland security responsibilities currently assigned to USNORTHCOM.

Summary

The creation of DHS and DoD restructuring in 2002 were historic and far reaching responses to correct the homeland security failures that were exploited by terrorists on 11 September 2001. There is no doubt that these institutions contributed greatly to the increased capabilities of the United States to provide homeland security to its populace. This is best demonstrated by the lack of a successful domestic terrorist attack on the United States, numerous responses to natural disasters, and the unimpeded execution of significant national events since 2001. While these institutions have served the national interest to great effect, the emergent threat posed by the national debt requires that greater efficiencies be found across the spectrum of the government. Consequently, we must find ways to increase the efficiency of the United States homeland security organizations because redundancy is a luxury we can no longer afford.

GLOSSARY

Homeland Defense. The protection of United States sovereignty, territory, domestic population, and critical defense infrastructure against external threats and aggression or other threats as directed by the President.

Homeland Security. A concerted national effort to prevent terrorist attacks within the United States; reduce America's vulnerability to terrorism, major disasters, and other emergencies; and minimize the damage and recover from attacks, major disasters, and other emergencies that occur.

National Defense. Any activity or effort performed to protect a nation against attack or other threats

National Security. Requirement to maintain the survival of the state through the use of economic, diplomatic, military, and political power.

BIBLIOGRAPHY

Books

Turabian, Kate L. *A Manual for Writers of Term Papers, Theses, and Dissertations.* 7th
ed. Revised by Wayne C. Booth, Gregory G. Colomb, Joseph M. Williams, and
the University of Chicago Press Editorial Staff. Chicago: University of Chicago
Press, 2007.

Periodicals

Barnett, Thomas P. M. "The Pentagon's New Map: It Explains Why We're Going to
War, and Why We'll Keep Going to War." *Esquire* (March 2003): 174.

Bellavita, Christopher. "Changing Homeland Security: What is Homeland Security?."
Homeland Security Affairs 4, Article 1 (June 2008). http://www.hsaj.org/
?article=4.2.1 (accessed 24 January 2012).

Government Documents

Mason, R. Chuck. *Securing America's Borders: The Role of the Military.* Washington
DC: Congressional Research Service, 16 June 2010. http://www.fas.org/
sgp/crs/index.html (accessed 28 March 2012).

Randol, Mark A. *Homeland Security Intelligence: Perceptions, Statutory Definitions, and
Approaches.* Washington DC: Congressional Research Service, 14 January 2009.
http://www.fas.org/sgp/crs/index.html (accessed 28 March 2012).

Senate Committee on Armed Services. Statement of General Charles H. Jacoby, Jr,
United States Army Commander United States Northern Command and North
American Aerospace Defense Command, 113th Cong., 13 March 2012.
http://www.armed-services.senate.gov/testimony.cfm?wit_id=10401&id=5265
(accessed 26 March 2012).

U.S. Commission on National Security/21st Century (Hart-Rudman Commission).
http://www.au.af.mil/au/awc/awcgate/nssg (accessed 2 December 2011).

U.S. Commission on National Security/21st Century. *New World Coming: American
Security in the 21st Century.* Washington, DC: Government Printing Office, 15
September 1999. https://www.fas.org (accessed 1 December 2011).

———. *Seeking A National Strategy: A Concert for Preserving Security and Promoting
Freedom.* Washington, DC: Government Printing Office, 15 April 2000.
https://www.fas.org (accessed 1 December 2011).

U.S. Department of Defense. *Fiscal Year 2013 Budget Request.* Washington DC: Government Printing Office, February 2012. http://comptroller.defense.gov/ budget2013.html (accessed 29 March 2012).

———. *Strategy for Homeland Defense and Civil Support.* Washington, DC: Government Printing Office, June 2005. http://www.defense.gov/ news/Jun2005/d20050630homeland.pdf (accessed 28 March 2012).

———. *The DoD Role in Homeland Security–Defense Study and Report To Congress.* Washington DC: July 2003. www.ndu.edu/uchs/ (accessed 28 March 2012).

U.S. Department of Homeland Security. *Bottom Up Review Report.* Washington, DC: Government Printing Office, July 2010. http://www.dhs.gov/xabout/ gc_1208534155450.shtm#0 (accessed 28 March 2012).

———. *Fiscal Year 2012 Budget Request–U.S. Department of Homeland Security(Overview).* Washington DC: Government Printing Office, 2012. http://www.dhs.gov/xabout/budget/dhs-budget.shtm (accessed 28 March 2012).

———. *FY13 Budget in Brief.* Washington DC: Government Printing Office. http://www.dhs.gov/xabout/budget/dhs-budget.shtm (accessed 28 March 2012).

———. *Homeland Security Organizational Chart.* Washington, DC: Government Printing Office. http://www.dhs.gov/ xabout/structure/editorial_0644.shtm (accessed 28 March 2012).

———. *National Response Framework.* Washington, DC: Government Printing Office, January 2008. http://www.fema.gov/emergency/nrf/ (accessed 21 March 2012).

———. *National Strategy for Homeland Security.* Washington, DC: Government Printing Office, July 2002. https://www.hsdl.org/homesec/docs/dhs/nps17-090605-05.pdf (accessed 2 December 2011).

———. *National Strategy for Homeland Security.* Washington, DC: Government Printing Office, October 2007. http://www.dhs.gov/xabout/history/ gc_1193938363680.shtm (accessed 2 December 2011).

———. *Quadrennial Homeland Security Review Report: A Strategic Framework for a Secure Homeland.* Washington. DC: Government Printing Office, February 2010. http://www.dhs.gov/xabout/ gc_1208534155450.shtm (accessed 28 March 2012).

U.S. Government Accountability Office. GAO Report 08-252, *Homeland Defense–Steps Have Been Taken to Improve U.S. Northern Command's Coordination with States and the National Guard Bureau, but Gaps Remain.* Washington, DC: Government Printing Office, April 2008. http://www.gao.gov (accessed 15 March 2012).

———. GAO Report 10-123, *Homeland Defense–Planning, Resourcing, and Training Issue Challenge DoD's Response to Domestic Chemical, Biological, Radiological, Nuclear, and High-Yield Explosive Incidents.* Washington, DC: Government Printing Office, October 2009. http://www.gao.gov (accessed 15 March 2012).

U.S. President. *National Security Presidential Directive 8.* http://www.sourcewatch.org/index.php?title=NSPD-8 (accessed 13 December 2011).

———. *Homeland Security Presidential Directive 8*, Annex 1. www.hsdl.org (accessed 13 December 2011).

———. *Presidential Decision Directive 39.* www.hsdl.org (accessed 2 December 2011).

———. *Presidential Policy Directive 8.* www.hsdl.org (accessed 2 December 2011).

———. *Presidential Study Directive 1.* www.hsdl.org (accessed 2 December 2011).

Other Sources

Carden, Michael J. "National Debt Poses Security Threat, Mullen Says." *American Forces Press Services*, 26 August 2010. www.jcs.mil/newsarticle.aspx?ID=360 (accessed 24 January 2012).

Constitution Project. "Potential Constitutional, Legal and Policy Issues Raised by a Unified Command for the Domestic United States: An Interim Report of the Constitution Project." http://www.constitutionproject.org/pdf/Northcom_Interim.pdf (accessed 27 March 2012).

Dobriansky, Paula J. "Threats to Security in the Western Hemisphere." Remarks at the Inter-American Defense College, Washington, DC, 20 October 2003.

Globalsecurity.org. "Eberhart Testimony at Confirmation Hearing, Advance Questions." http://www. globalsecurity.org/military/library/congress/2002_hr/eberhart620.pdf (accessed 15 January 2012).

Murdock, Clark, Pierre Chao, Anne A. Witkowsky, Michele A. Flournoy, Christine E. Wormuth, Mac Bollman, Jeremiah Gertler, Adam N. Marks, Noah J. Richmond, David R. Scruggs, and Richard Weitz. *Beyond Goldwater-Nichols: U.S. Government and Defense Reform for a New Strategic Era–Phase 2 Report.* Washington, DC: Center for Strategic and International Studies, July 2005. http://csis.org/publication/beyond-goldwater-nichols-phase-ii-report (accessed 27 March 2012).

Shelstad, Kristine L. "The Domestic Security Command–The Evolution of the U.S. Northern Command." Master's Thesis, Naval Postgraduate School, Monterrey, CA, 2011.

USNORTHCOM.mil. http://www.northcom.mil/About/index.html (accessed 27 March 2012).

Vrooman, Stephen. "Homeland Security Strategy from the Cold War into the Global War on Terrorism: An Analysis of Deterrence, Forward Presence, and Homeland Defense." Master's Thesis, U.S. Army. Command and General Staff College, Ft. Leavenworth, KS, 2004.

Whittaker, Alan, Frederick C. Smith, and Elizabeth McKune. *The National Security Policy Process: The National Security Council and Interagency System.* Washington, DC: Industrial College of the Armed Forces, National Defense University, U.S. Department of Defense, 15 August 2011.